I0162254

First Breath

2010 Savant Anthology of Poems

Edited by
Zachary M. Oliver

Savant Books
Honolulu, HI, USA
2010

Published in the USA by Savant Books and Publications
2630 Kapiolani Blvd #1601
Honolulu, HI 96826
http://www.SavantBooksAndPublications.com

Printed in the USA

Edited by Zachary M. Oliver
Cover Photos and Design by Daniel S. Janik

10 digit ISBN: 0-9845552-2-6
13-digit ISBN: 978-0-9845552-2-2

Dedication

As the editor of the first Savant Poetry Anthology, I send this modest work out into the world, encouraging people everywhere to play a little more - in this case with the savory, sensory images hidden inside of everyday words.

- Zachary M. Oliver

Table of Contents

<u>She</u>
Daniel S. Janik

It is raining
Thunderclouds.
Let us go for a drive
This Sunday raining
Against the winds
Beyond the speed of sounds
Deep
And deeper
Into self
Deep
Into the rain
Of Sundays.
Deep into the thunderclouds
Of yesteryears.

Daniel S. Janik is an award-winning poet with poems appearing in sixteen books throughout the world. Author of "Footprints, Smiles and Little White Lies" (Savant 2008), "The Illustrated Middle Earth" (Savant 2008) and "Last and Final Harvest" (Savant 2008), he has penned over 60 books and publications including "Unlock the Genius Within" (Rowman and Littlefied 2005), "How to Choose the Best English Language School in the USA" (AuthorHouse 2005), "Sourdough Scott's Bedtime Fairy Tales from Alaska" (Publication Consultants 2006), and "A Whale's Tale" (Savant 2009).

<u>Waltzing with King</u>
Erin L George

Aaaaah! My striking Diamond
our souls have not only met
but intertwined at fire burning sunsets
and curled beneath the full moon.
Do you not remember?
Did you forget?
We danced among the constellations
a quintillion years ago.

Nooooooo! You are mistaken, my crazy King
our souls have never touched
or had yet the chance to waltz
and sleep in the shadows of stars.
Do you not know? Do you not see?
Had we danced or had we ever met
the force would have been far, far too great
for us to ever separate!

Silence! My beautiful ancient one.
Did you not feel the swirling of the angels' symphony?
Have you forgotten of our supreme guidance?
She induced our spin in energies unknown
for if you and I could find our way back
our souls were meant to be:
and so it is, unbreakable love.
Do you not feel infinity in our oneness?
We did indeed, dance a waltz
and slept in the shadows of the stars
just underneath the first of history.

The question is:
Will you, again, join me?

to Kwesi

∞

Erin L George is a freelance writer from southern New Hampshire. George has had several poems and articles published in journals, anthologies and magazines since 1995. She has received numerous awards from the New England Press Association for her work as a journalist. She recently self-published a book of poetry, Dandelion Dance, and is currently working on a second, Insideout.

<u>On the Birth of Simplicity</u>
Zachary M. Oliver

She smiles from the thought-child
pregnant
inside her. While not quite ready for this
world, she knows it mingles with:
her heartbeat,
blood, and
love.

For years, she
fluttered through life on a
light impulse breeze.
She toyed with too-cool magazine
fashion,
New-Age rhetoric,
and green Earth passion

Not anymore.
Stroking her belly, she smiles. Her thoughts
nurturing the
spiritual love-child
moving inside, she pauses
for a peaceful moment imagining curled-up
fingers and toes.

Soon, her thought-child will
Push, pause, and push again.
Stunned and shocked, the moment will arrive and
painfully cry the mystic truth:
"To find

simplicity,
we need to know more."

Zachary Oliver EdD continually searches for his niche in life. He believes in living life always prepared to learn and share. Basking the beautiful sunshine and cool trade winds, he shares his life with his beautiful ohana and awesome students. Currently authoring a book, he is sketching some ideas about learning and coloring these ideas with vibrant stories about his decade in the classroom.

<u>Rain and More than Love</u>
Gabjirel Ra

In bed when once you were born,
now is the time to lie with the stars;
shall we be the victims or just are we going to
cry the diamonds out from our hearts;
it's not the dream when we sleep,
it's more than reality and less than blessing,
I'm giving the words and stealing the voice,
one is the bird that I curse;
ashes it's not my rebirth,
cruel and unveiling, tempting and glittering;
past is the tear from the blind eye;
it is I that have been here always,
it is I that tormented virgins with gold phalluses,
it is I that have been ruling with never born children,
Buddha saw the pain, Buddha saw the pleasure of creation;
those who are in between mercury thought and
those who are the creators of the gold;
my king is deep in the woods,
my queen is deep under the waters.
 Save me, save me from my impure movements!

Give me love and give me the poison made of the holy blood;
rising and falling and no more naked imprisoning of modern
mind,
there is the truth and there is the symbol of sublimation,
destruction is my loveliest hug from the mother.

Innocent as a world and guilty as an individual.

No more shall we be the dancing dolls on the fashion integrity,
I don't have answers or the questions just animal urge;
I don't believe in death and have no fear of my own touch,
is this the terror when somebody is forced to die or just
the mercy for the weak once;
air is the color and fire is the destiny,
spirit rejoicing with no existence;
in bed when once you were born,
there is the solution and there is the memory,
for all the future sounds of pleasures,
under the earth my indifference is blooming.

Is our savior androgynous machine?
And we are nothing more than hopes of what we could be;
becoming and blindly trusting,
for all who are in love with me, hate comes as a good
justification for every kindness;
I will be free to feel, but never as much as it's expected;
everything is transmission of energy and martyrdom;
hesitation if I ask for gender, but angel has the wings,
that's all that he has.

If I'm shallow, how could I distinguish myself from you;
there is a better world inside of this one,
but it has no gates,
I have marred my reflection from the mirror,
I have divorced myself from unpleasant sound situations,
and the maiden and the godlike stone,

First Breath

I have one face divided by two Suns;
all in all as one in plenty
I'm invoking my father,
father of all emotions as mystical floods of new eon.
Do I hear the screams or that's just the song of celebration
cosmos of understanding when heavens are in the labour
one drop of rain and more than love.

Gabrijel Savic Ra *(1978), Belgrade born multimedia artist, poet and art theorist. Studied philosophy at Belgrade Philosophical Faculty. As a multimedia artist participate in many worldwide exhibitions and festivals. He has published two books of poetry: Power Of The Fallen Angel (2002) and Last Lovers (2003) and contributed to many magazines and anthologies (Scriptures 26 and 27, Remont Art Magazine, Alma's Collection Of Best Short Stories For 2005, Word In Space, BAP Quarterly, Language And Culture...).*

To pay the heart no mind
Is to welcome love's depart
And no lesson's learned in time
If the mind is paid no heart

A Breath
Helen Doan

I've lapsed and lost before
Footings to infinity
Falling from the open arms
That cannot comfort me

Giving into hope, I failed
With tainted shame, drew back
It broke my spirit, left me frail
Adds to everything I lacked

High prospects were to me
What meek winds are to kite
That hoist it half to sea
To land its sail... mid-flight.

If such is but a choice
Who would lust the acrid pain?
Giving air to breathless voice
Holding on to worthless gains?

So long as heartaches would
Stand their trial ground, attest,
Ears are deaf, unmoved by words
Disheartened so by emptiness.

Yet those unaltered words

Rapt every meaning true
Listened to as they are heard
When spoken plain by you

I could never more surmise
Crestfallen hands of death
Or live in drear disguise
To give or take a breath

For your love has been to me
What moon is to the night
My Love, you are to me
What sunlight is to life

And if I am truly yours
I feel honored just to be
Half the person that you are...
The person you've become to me.

❧

Helen Doan is a Vietnamese-American writer born in Kien Giang, Vietnam in 1981 and came to San Jose, California in 1986 where she grew up. Poetry was her first love since grade school and writing it became an undying passion in the years ahead. Endeavoring to become a screenwriter, Doan moved from the Bay Area to Southern California in 2002 where she spent over eight years writing feature-length screenplays and keeping a diary of her independence. Currently living and working in the county of Los Angeles, Doan aspires to become a full-fledged screen and novel writer with the release of "On My Behalf" (anticipated Summer 2010 release). Author website at http://www.helendoan.com

Pampering Cradle
V. Bright Saigal

Blowing from the west, thee murmuring;
Waking up the laughter of ripples
Fragrance pampering my heart,
As the cradle song once saddled before;
Western breeze murmuring, when the blossom shying away,
Happiness blossomed once again
Far off at the bottom in my heart,
Turning the sky red, behind blue and vibrant
Deeply weeping the day falling once again,
Bidding farewell, warbling birds filled in the jungle
Darkness swallowing the once and again,
Smiling crescent behind the hills peeped again
Winking stars strewn across the sky smiling,
Weeping my heart still waiting,
Those pampering cradle once I laid.

to My Mother

*Being the eldest son of labor class parents, who had no formal education, **V. Bright Saigal** had to work hard to earn for books. His mother used to stitch his old clothes to extend their life, and the patches of poverty can still be found on every corner of his life. Two months school vacation was no break, it was time to generate funds for the new academic year. A single pair of dress pants supported him throughtout his two years of intermediate school. Five rupees per day, his part time job fed him. His head unloaded thousands of cement bags. Determination made him a monolith. Public libraries made him a graduate. He had to sleep, many days in cold winter. Still, he came out of INDIAN INSTITUTE OF MASS COMMUNICATION, Asia's best of its kind.*

Exogenicity
Daniel S. Janik

If there does exist
Love
My dear
I say
My dear
Then it was born on your lips
From the vocal cords of your heart
Not a breath
But said in the rhythm of your momentary stare.

My words are phantoms of the space
Between
My dear
I say
My dear
They vibrate and twist
Like dark thunderclouds
About tavern gas-lamps
Searching out holes in the molding.

Never have I known a midnight fog
So dense it can soak into the bone
As fast as a casually tossed word.

Blind the eyes
Hope
My dear
I say
My dear

Flames fixed on church candles
On alters of midnight Easter mass
Their radiance but a barrier
To the light I carry.

Love
Words
Light
My dear
I say
My dear
There is no place so dark
You or your love can pretend to crawl out
From beneath the hovering phantoms of my words.

<u>Unnamed</u>
Daniel S. Janik

The sun,
God's plaything,
The evening,
His toy box. Kana.

<u>Light</u>
Francis H Powell

A light extinguished
Light in the distance
Turn to the light
Light at the end of a conversation
Attracted by light
Confused by light
Light entering a dark corridor
Light entering a passage in time
Light around the corner
Light filling spaces
A troubling light
Light cutting through the darkness
Light needed for survival
The light of confusion

My light
Your light
Drowning in light
Light disturbs me
The light of knowledge
Extended light on a summers day
Lack of light in a northern territory
Hope spread by light
Faltering light
Light eternal
Light never ending
False light
Neon light
Natural light

The light of stars
Breaking light
White light
Flickering light
Light spreads hope

⊗

Born in 1961, in Reading, England. Educated at various schools before going on to art school to do a degree in painting and an MA in printmaking. Early working life included jobs working with children and young adults, in London. While in Austria, he began to write stories. Moved back to England, where upon pursued teaching career, including teaching English (literature/language) and art. Decided to move to France at the end of 1999.

Working for IFG Langue, as an English teacher for the past eight years, as well as having exhibitions in Paris and doing concerts in Paris area, as well as a festival in Seville, May 2006. Also a poet, who has had works published, in poetry magazines, as well as work published on the internet. As a writer, he has had four short stories published in magazine, "Rat Mort" a magazine with dark and surreal stories. 2006 has also seen him publish various articles on the internet, and a new job, sending a monthly Arts report on Paris arts culture, for the "Bohemian aesthetic".
http://www.patsymoore.com/bohemians/PLA1.html
Short story "mutant" published "Freakwave" magazine 2008
Short story "sans defaut" published 2008 empreintes (translation of "Flawless")
Has also had short stories and poetry published on another American site "Multi-dimensions"
One of these stories had 27,000 views (for a story called "purged") according to the site.
http://www.multidimensions.net/PeopleTalk/PeopleTalk.php

<u>I Am</u>
Orest Stocco

I felt ashamed of life when I saw her frail body
fighting for its life in the Emergency Room,
emaciated, and heaving like a bellows for air;
I saw no dignity in the physical struggle
to stay alive, no grace, no love, no honor,
just a bodily organism in the throes of death.
I walked home alone from the hospital,
the lonely moon as big as the Eye of God
and the stars sparkling like lost souls in heaven,
and I thought of life and death and everything
in between, and in my heart I smiled for all
of my efforts, struggles, and humiliations to find
my true self, because as I spied death steal my lover's
mother's life I knew, I simply knew, that I am,
and life is merely something that I do.

Orest Stocco, *author of the provocative novel, "What Would I Say Today If I Were To Die Tomorrow?" was born in Panettieri, Calabria, Italy. He immigrated to Canada and studied philosophy at university. He lived in Annecy, France and northwestern Ontario before taking up residence in Georgian Bay, Ontario, Canada, where he continues to write novels, short stories and poetry. His novel, "My Unborn Child" is in the process of being published, with a release date of May, 2010, by Savant Books and Publications, Honolulu, Hawaii.*

Who could be as sage, fair and true
As the ego subsisting in you?

Burgeoning when needs are met
And flourishing as it is fed!

Thence, never feel less wonderful
Or none may follow through...
Know yourself as beautiful
And they shall see it too.

PERFECT
Helen Doan

Ask Stars if they are perfect
As our highest form of light
Ask why they shy away
Light-years into the night

Ask Pearls where they are from
And what molded them to be
Ask if they view themselves
As treasures of the sea

Ask Diamonds if they're flawless
And Wine, if it is pure...
Ask Rubies if they've noticed
The envy of their peers

Ask Fairytales and Fables
Whoever thought them up
Ask Stars and Pearls and Diamonds

...before they question us.

GORILLA IN A STOREFRONT WINDOW
Scott Mastro

The road came out of the forest and tried to cross the
highway
Where the gorilla swung in his store-front window
Making it difficult to keep your attention to traffic,
Wanting to see what the big ape would do
If you slowed down
As you drove by wondering
What the gorilla would be doing
As soon as you were out of sight.

*Former journalist, public educator and other mind-numbing incarnations too ghastly to mention, **Scott Mastro** has lived all over the place and continues to do so. Other Savant titles: "Tales from Two Sides of the Atlantic."*

<u>Sufi Sausages</u>
Orest Stocco

The best sausages that I ever tasted
are made from a secret Sufi recipe that I found one day
while looking for the Way.

I was so hungry for God that I would have eaten anything
to preserve my spiritual strength; and I did, a cult
concoction

of sun and nonsense that gave me spiritual cramps for
many years.

Then I chanced upon a Sufi sausage maker who gave me
a secret recipe that changed my life forever.

"You take the casing that you have," he instructed me,
"and stuff

it with the meat of the last supper."

I had no idea what he meant, until I re-read the Christian
Bible;

and from the moment I caught the Light that Jesus
shone,

I discerned the Sufi sausage maker's wisdom, and I
began

to practice the sacred art of Sufi sausage making.

The first few batches that I made were much too spicy,

because I stuffed my casing with every esoteric meat
that I could find;

but with time, patience, and an ardent desire for God,
I learned to stuff my casing with the freshest meat of all,
the tender

flesh of my own simple, daily life. And the more I died to
my mortal flesh,

the sweeter my sausages tasted, and the more strength I
gathered

for my long journey back home to God.

Those Old Days
V Bright Saigal

Those old days, have gone
Leaving, rays of memory behind
Never ending hope, still in my horizon
Living in me, spreading the rays of hope
Will you come one day? Showering
Happiness and smile, giving me a hand
Every little moment, sparks in my heart
Igniting, the past and you
I am still in love, with those days
You showered in my heart and on me
Rise again, from the silence
Giving me a hope, still, I await
The never-ending thirst of love
Still, roaring in my heart
Breaking four walls, of this world and mine
Will you come one day?

Strange and Different
Francis H. Powell

I have never been to India
but I feel like I have breathed
in the air, conversing with a maharaja
While on an elephant sozzled with gin
I have pranced on a delicate leaf
written poems and shaved my head
I have never thrown a rotten tomato
at a politician on a podium
or carrots at an insolent donkey.
Nor have I run with a pack of hyenas
or counted up all my misdemeanors.
I have always painted with a fullness of heart
and respected others despite divisions
My mind has drifted to Africa, and dust filled Somalia
I have shivered in Siberia and sweated in Egypt.
When I depart this world,
my head will be filled with memories
of places and people strange and different

The Guru of Angst
Orest Stocco

Dressed in black with short cropped hair,
he milks the udder of despair. A poet, singer,
lover, and thief he churns the sour milk of life
into pure gold and lives like a lavish prince.
With a haunting voice he sings of the pain that
people want to hear, confirming their misery
and robbing them of every hope of being free.
He drinks red wine for breakfast and beds
groupies because he can, and to ease his ennui
he flees to a secluded monastery to study the
ancient teaching of the selfless self; and when
he has had his fill of the selfless life he returns
with new poems to sing and reaffirms his icon
status as the popular guru of angst.

Ne Me Quitte Pas
Gabjirel Ra

I love death because it erases choice possibility
I love to be undecided because only
then I'm certain,
I love long hollow conversations and
sleepless nights spent with
my friends,
scattered cigarette smoke and
half empty glass,
Rimbaud and Kandinsky,
reverie under the paleness of the day,
I love my wife and her
colorless aristocratic skin,
reminiscence of the past and
ignorance of the future,
all the moments with family and
their embracing acceptance,
I love morning coffee,
with sensitiveness inundate poem,
I love the phone because I don't see
but only hear the voice,
walk next to the river and Heraclitus,
everlasting change as
the ultimate self-consciousness,
I love first spring flowers and
mint tea,
I love freshness and
purity of greetings with
people I once knew,
I love French singer and

fact that I understand the words
of the song,
I love the hand of the beggar on
the main street and his smile,
I love boring curator in the gallery,
drunk penman and
vainness of human kind,
I love death because it erases choice possibility
the verity that when I die,
I will disappear forever.

<u>Ripples of Love</u>
V Bright Saigal

Ripples of love never subside,
Till the graveyard honor, and beyond
Sun and stars, smile and wink,
Yet, the showering tears, and smile prevail
Blurred vision and weeping heart mourn,
Before you lay silent, and beyond
The ocean of love, and legacy, prevail,
You left behind, and far
Leaving behind the day's memories,
Hugging me still, the fragrance of past
Smile once, as you did ever,
From this coffin, before you leave

<u>Song for Super-Sane</u>
Zachary M. Oliver

Spinning hair
into
woven locks of dread, he
snagged and snarled:
Thinking of the lions roaring in his
ear, the tortured spirit conjuring them, and phantom
fulfillment
always lurking near.

Wearily, in the midst of the chaos
he tipped his
chin
to the sky and fixed his
tired eyes as if to say: "I am ready to make my
journey; fill me with
light! Let me fly!"

But, there was no light or
grace: no
phosphorescent flash or sonic boom.
Instead, Super-Sane heard a
whisper from just beyond the noise which said:
"The silence you seek is born of
balance."

They say the eyes reflect the soul
And skies made oceans blue
In truth, they should have known
That this beauty came from you

A Rose
Helen Doan

She smiles sensuously
Eyes wrinkling with her age
Winter flirts about her stance
How so her hair has grayed!

In a fair and gallant stride
She greets the world anew
And dances before heaven
Like an angel before you

She drew in sentiments
In trance before her eyes
With a heart so passion-fed
That time can't pass her by

Now memories' all she has
Within a heart and soul
As goodness tends to last
When youth and beauty go

Yet a girl, she remains
Happy and unafraid

As a rose remains a rose
By any other shade.

A Bouquet of Wild Flowers
Orest Stocco

She asked me to check the bread-maker this morning,
which has a tendency to not knead the dough
completely,

but I got lost deep in thought as I wrote my daily poem
(I blame Robert Bly for this), and I forgot. I went to work
upon completing my poem (Bly doesn't have a day job),
but when I came home for coffee I smelled the bread
and

remembered what I was supposed to do. I opened the
bread-maker door expecting to see a heavenly loaf nicely
baking, but instead my eyes beheld an ugly lump of
dough

struggling for integrity, and guilt possessed me. I left the
loaf to bake, hoping some miracle would make it rise, but
just in case the God of bread did not hear my prayer I
stopped on my way home for lunch and picked a
bouquet

of wild flowers. When I walked into the house I heard the
disappointment in her voice as she called my name, but
before she told me about the bread I handed her the
cheerful bouquet and said, "I forgot and I'm sorry and
these

are for you." Her face lit up with love, as it always does

when I surprise her the way I do, and when she left for
work

again she smiled and said to me, "You're such a joy to
live

with. I'll put on a fresh loaf when I get home."

Hard Times
Daniel S. Janik

Hard times
We spread
Like butter
On our bread crusts.
Worry
The bitter hops we drink
To wash away the aftertaste.
With concrete placenta
And steel umbilical cord
The new world feeds her unborn
Discontent
We remember
The plastic smiles,
The cold, uncaring hands
The bitter gall we fed upon
And other feces of the Revolution.
They have no place
In this new world
Of florescent green, electric blood!

Salad City
Francis H. Powell

Nobody can breathe in Salad City
There's snakes in the sea, in salad city
They are just living out a dream in Salad City
Or just throwing their lives away

I went there when I was twenty one
Just wanted to live a bit, and have some fun
I was caught in the crossfire of a city at war
There was harmony and hell in the midst of it all

You can't sail in the breeze in Salad city
There are toxic trees in salad city
The children are searching for fields to play
and the mayor is attached to the end of a chain

There are people sitting on cactus pins,
trying to atone for their faults and sins
All the shop keepers love to scowl and frown
And the taxi drivers, drive with their eyes to the ground

La Cumbia
Scott Mastro

Everyone at the buffet
Would rather be making love,

Eating their way to orgasm in cheap straw hats,

Dreaming tequila dances with Hispanic young girls.

The band finishes and packs
Something from the buffet,

Loads the bus and drives,

Leaving the rest of us to decide among those at the
buffet.

Conversing with the Voices
Erin L. George

Aaaaah, my sweet sugar cane,
your spell have those around me contemplating,
if I have gone completely insane,
maybe so, I should lay across a couch,
and share my love for you with a shrink,
I will gladly be other than normal,
while my ink fantasies, are manifested into solid realities,
by you as you give me the rock solid wink.

Arrgh, but fear not my refugee
For I am caught in a bubble
Bouncing and spinning on tangerine
Dreams, I should wake up! So they say.
I will gladly ricochet across moon beams,
Stitching rainbow smiles in my song,
If only to sing it for you –
To be heard by you and never to pop.

Galactic equations of neuronal spill out
orgasmic atomic bubbles escaping from my nape
your taste is greater than strawberry ice cream pink
I sink deep in the fullness of your refugee
stuffed and equated to your song
I too, will never pop.

Trapped in Crap
Scott Mastro

Everything in this place is half-ass-rigged-together
like drunken dry-wallers

leaving unfinished faux-stucco walls for an angry
carpenter to touch up with a crescent wrench.

On Fear
Zachary M. Oliver

Unconsciously putting his
head into the
path of a wild
fist following fear-filled
stink-eye, the
youth
knew nothing: not the "how," the
"what" or "why." He only
felt it
smash. Not so young, he didn't
cry.

Cradling his
sucker-punched soul, an
idea made its way through the
headache and damaged
pride: "Let it go," it said,
"Anger is
nothing, but an
aggressive
expression of
fear."

I've cheated every sense
To stake my standing tall
When in blatant foolishness
It is I who done befall.

Secrets
Helen Doan

Secrets jeered in wicked ways
Shrouding yet, its gaudy bluff
Feigning knowledge without say
Of when is quite enough

For how are they untold
And be not question-prone?
When all we live to know
Are never truly known?

Such are the mists of fear
Enveloping like steam
The lave of cloud nine tears
For moments unredeemed

And to feel as I have felt!
Set freed from all pretense
Just once, I told myself
...repeatedly again.

To be in vain pursuit
Of vast togetherness
Or of seconds that induced
The forsaking of the rest

To know that love is blind
In the breathing of your name
And heart is filled with sights
That vision cannot claim

Yet when the time spurred forth
Two pulses ran remote
Like one to withered hearth
I clung to ailing hope

For another chance to hear
Your mellow tone of voice
Which, like rhapsody to ear,
Could drown the heap of noise

I shall forgo resistance
That sequestered me at bay
For my only odds with distance
Keeps you but a dream away

So I may hold you closer
And the clock might tarry still
The cold will turn no colder
And wind shall send no chill

But short we are of compromise
That satiates enough
The craze of famished cries
In the appetite of love

Even murmurs' slow to speak

Of how contentment feels
As when secrets failed to keep
What silence meant to seal

Once more to have attempt
The quest for answers tough
Perhaps I'll grasp again
That never is enough.

Not So Very High
Jack Howard

Higher than I might climb
Limbs against a winter sky
Branching forms of past
Summer births did so try

Over hilly shouldered mount
There, far up is feather mind
Taller, higher than I may see
Not merely for eyes to find

Redoubt must be soul's home
Mind below cannot unwind
So I will follow some sense
Child, imitating my own kind

Ere I believe I will forgetful be
Till in fulfilling the quiet heart
Not nearly sunset so very high
Love will be my sky's own part

Jack Howard *was born, to his great advantage, in a small fishing village called Ilwaco, Washington. With a BA in history, trained as a lawyer, pounding the streets as a news reporter, he served, in his second life, as a post-secondary teacher in paralegal studies, English (his favorite subject), business and writing. Interests in federal Indian law led him to work with several Washington State Puget Sound tribes. God's greatest blessings in his life are three wonderful children (Jackson, Sophie, and ZZ), and a passion for radio theater, horses, oceans, and North Dakota.*

Sunday not Monday
Francis H Powell

The sound of the bells cracks open the sky
Your raven black hair cascades
to the clutches of your shoulders
There are no murmurs from the street
the city has not found its feet
There's the trash from the night before
a discarded sandwich from "Subway"
a multitude of bottles
piled up, in pyramid forms
Anglers perch over a river of contaminated fish
While joggers weave past old ladies
with petulant dogs, free from constraint
and crusty tired eyes connect
and conversations are enacted in bleary tones
Your yawn is another ode to your exhaustion
from the passage of a previous week.
We are owned by our jobs
the tasks we are forced to do
but then there is Sunday.

First Breath

If you enjoyed *First Breath* consider these other fine Books
from Savant Books and Publications:

Poetry Books:
Last and Final Harvest by Daniel S. Janik
The Illustrated Middle Earth by Daniel S. Janik
Footprints, Smiles and Little White Lies by Daniel S. Janik

Prose Books:
Kanaka Blues by Mike Farris
Called Home by Gloria Schumann
The Bahrain Conspiracy by Bentley Gates
Today I Am A Man by Larry Rodness
The Interzone by Tatsuyuki Kobayashi
Dare to Love in Oz by William Maltese
The Village Curtain by Tony Tame
Tropic of California by R. Page Kaufman
A Whale's Tale by Daniel S. Janik

Scheduled for Release in 2010:
Poor Rich by Jean Blasiar
The Jumper Chronicles by W. C. Peever
Mythical Voyage by Robin Ymer
Ammon's Horn by Guerrino Amati
My Unborn Child by Orest Stocco

If you are a poet or writer and would like to be published
contact Savant Books and Publications at
http://www.savantbooksandpublications.com